IN THE HOUSE IN THE WOODS

ROSEANNA ALICE BOSWELL

IN THE HOUSE IN THE WOODS

Cooper Dillon

In the House | In the Woods

Copyright © 2024 Roseanna Alice Boswell

All rights reserved. First Edition

Cooper Dillon Books
San Diego, California
CooperDillon.com

Cover & Interior Design by Adam Deutsch

ISBN: 978-1-943899-21-0

For my sisters, here and gone, and for my mother

Table of Contents

I. *How to Trace Your Daughtering*

I REALLY NEED A RAINSTORM	1
QUEEN ANNE'S LACE	2
TO MY SISTER ON HER TWENTY-THIRD:	4
THE ANIMAL, AGAIN	5
GIVING OR GUTTING	6
WATERCOLORS	8
ELEGY FOR MY BODY IMAGINED	10
SELF-PORTRAIT AS A MANY-SUNNED THING	11
I DREAM MY BROTHER TELLS ME HE WAS WRONG	16
BEREAVEMENT RATES	18
I DON'T KNOW HOW TO TELL YOU THAT YOU DIDN'T PREPARE ME FOR THE REAL WORLD	20
THE HEARTTHROBS OF MY GIRLHOOD	22
EVERY TIME I HAVE A BIRTHDAY & SYLVIA PLATH DOESN'T	24
TWO MONTHS AFTER MY SISTER'S FUNERAL, I WAKE	26
I WANT TO SAVE YOU FROM YOURSELF BUT INSTEAD I WRITE POEMS ABOUT AN ANIMAL SWALLOWING THE SUN WHOLE	28
ON SEEING ONE BABY SHOE IN THE ALDI PARKING LOT	30
SUGARING SEASON	31
IF I HAVE A DAUGHTER, I WILL CALL HER *SHIPWRECK*	32

WHEN A STRANGER CALLS THINKING I'M HER SISTER	34
UNSAYING GHOSTS	36
UNSAYING MY OWN HEART	38
SHELL WITH BOG & GHOST	39
SELF-PORTRAIT AS MY SISTER'S FRECKLE	40
ACKNOWLEDGMENTS	54

I.

How to Trace Your Daughtering

I REALLY NEED A RAINSTORM

Oklahoma summer   & sweat skim   all my flowers

are dying   heat stroke leaves   I know

suffering when it snakes   around stem-necks

my grief plant   condolence gift   might not make

it   might die   how sad/funny   how fitting

the sun   always portrayed   as male

consumes everything   my porch   graveyard

a small amuse-bouche   I could smother

the heat   my twist-bed   twist-sheets

the box fan   circulating the same   air forever

QUEEN ANNE'S LACE

I see them along the highway for miles before I recognize them—
their white crowns dip up & down on spindled stems, delicate
carrot-top leaves. The Adirondack Mountains dip up & down
beneath me. I try to unsee a dead coyote.

Returns are like this—swallowing
the fear that the mountain is trying to buck me from it
& lap up the dizzy view instead. Glut my eyes on flowers.
Drive another forty miles.

I have never written an origin story before.   That's not true.

I have never written one I could corroborate. My memories
swan dive from car windows, even when I am with my sisters
& we say remember when remember when as if there were a
    balloon-tether
that could hold us. A dandelion chain for wishes, or else.

It goes like this:

*I am driving home to see my mother & it is mid-July / I am driving home
& there are flowers on the highway / I am driving up 81
North & the flowers are Queen Anne's Lace / I picked them for fairies
when I was small / There is a dead coyote but I don't see it / I do*

*see the coyote but he is alive, an omen / The coyote is dead & I see
his furred bones / I wonder if the fairies will eat or bury him.*

I have five sisters & they all played pretend with me on the farm
we grew up on in Northern NY. No one believes the beginning
of this story, the part where we are born in the woods
& stayed there. Found fairy circles & left them undisturbed
& unsalted. I come home to visit & I think the trees have
missed me. I feel a gnawing in my bark-bones
I try to pretend I missed them, too.

The road is still light & the toll booths are counting
—tell me to hurry, hurry, hurry across another county, another
rivered town. My mother calls to tell me to hurry
safely. My sisters are waiting for me & I am close.
I will beat the dark this time but still watch for deer
along the side of the road, imagine their knees
in the stems & grass. I'm sure they can scent death on the fur,
the pixie-joy of a roadside burial. My headlights
do a small dance on the coyote's bones as I exit.

TO MY SISTER ON HER TWENTY-THIRD:

Remember when we played Barbies, even after I was grown?
I wonder where those dolls are now, what landfill
they accessorize. Who makes them talk and talk out of
pastel smiles with no teeth. Which one ended up bagging
Ken. You prop your phone against the mirror
while we video chat so I can help you select an outfit
—match shoes to leopard pencil skirt. I watch you consider
yourself. Smooth a hand over stomach, then hips, then hair:
a wandering inventory coming up wanting. I found
an old picture of me on Facebook I won't show you. In it
I am bending away from the camera—hiding thighs and arms,
the dip between my breasts and waist. I have used other words
for shame to gloss our girlhoods. Said self-conscious or shy instead.
Built a mythos out of changing clothes five times before dinner.
I remember eating these alone in the kitchen after leaving
the table—spoon dipping straight from the pot to feel
the pressure of *enough* against my stomach. I wish I could tell you
when we outgrow this.

THE ANIMAL, AGAIN

When I can't sleep I tell myself the sun
can't be swallowed forever. Whatever
is consumed reemerges. I tell myself
the story about the animal in the woods,
revise it over & over:

*There never was a beast. He never swallowed the sun
that summer. Heat didn't curl off trees
turn to smoke in my hair & eyes. I still miss
the house, woods leaning in to taste windows.*

In the dark, my cat pads softly across carpet
looking for bugs or other prey to practice on.
These are his night sounds. I try to get it right:

*If the beast swallowed the sun, he coughed it up
       on forest floor—streaming morning air.
The sun dragged like wet feathers at first
       but still rose: pale & certain-skyed.*

My husband breathes next to me. A moth
beats himself dully against my window.
The cat has settled between our feet
at the bottom of our bed. When he yawns
I think I see a yellow glint of wings.

GIVING OR GUTTING

Find me operatic. Imagine me orgasmic
screamware—filmy & beckoning. I am
everything you always knew you deserved,

aren't I? Sometimes when I lie on my back
I imagine playing my ribcage like a mandolin
—round-bellied wood sound crooning. My

cream skin. My largeness. I am always
turning a phrase with my tongue tip
because I am in the business of oracle

& fish bone. What excuse is there for being
a poet. A soft flaying of everything I touch,
but I won't justify myself. I'll just open

a little wider. Tell you something you already
know but make it hurt so good—
that's what I'm known for. That's my sweet

spot. That's how you know I'm carving
up something really special: a shivering
piece of flesh to wrap in gauze or paper

& still. Divining this poem feels too easy
because what have I risked, really? Too much
of myself is always following behind me

my own shadow, my own wings,
my own my own my own.

WATERCOLORS

I go to the museum to find paintings of bodies

    dimple-fleshed women looking

over a shoulder   under a leaf

    an impossible glow touches them all

a private sun I can't look

    away from   When I was a girl

my mother showed me a watercolor

    book on sex   the space between the man

& the woman was a tender shadow

    I imagined what was hiding there

a smooth sweep of skin   animaled

    & wild   the brushing sound

a coat makes when you walk

      or something cold melting   Names

of parts were a soft annotation

    a small afterthought   I learn later

to chart myself with a hand mirror

    look for shade   & find layers

place a curatorial sign to house each one

    At the museum   I come to stare

wonder if the women ever close

    their eyes & think of snow

ELEGY FOR MY BODY IMAGINED

In photos you can tell my grandmother was
a dancer. She leans from the frame, toes turned
out, arm arced over her head. My mother looks

the same—boned shoulders like delicate fish
ribs, hands soft & small. I wore her wedding dress
when I was 11, lace overlay hugging my waist

perfectly. Skirt falling over my feet. I hoped
I would only grow taller: develop slight hips,
small breasts. I grew fast after that. My period

arriving in a February snowfall, my hips unfolding
like a monstrous cardboard cutout. Breasts & fat
& thighs all overspilling corners. I became

unlike overnight. Hunger resting heavy on my clavicles,
desire curving my belly-folds into a kind of shame
I could pinch at. Who would know where I came from

—how would they trace my daughtering. I try
to find the outline of her in my spine. The place I end
& she begins. In the sharpness of sunlight

I see her willowing in my shadow. I bend an arm
& let her pose.

SELF-PORTRAIT AS A MANY-SUNNED THING

[in the house]

I accidentally break my mother's
curved bottle of perfume, top
all lip & pout. I smash it on blue
linoleum floor. I just wanted
to hold it for a minute, maybe
less. Breathe a little bit of grown-up.
Catch my own reflection, mothered.

[in the yard]
I'm at the pump-handle again,
slice of sunburn watermelon-red
across my legs, washing the dirt off
my feet while the sky squats bow-legged,
daring anyone to call her a tomboy.
I know the look of a daughter grown
too long. The way light dances off
glass & makes smaller suns,
clumsy or angry.

[in the barn]

The tortoiseshell cat has another litter
of kittens behind a hay bale. I spy
on them through dust moats, name
each shape as they nose blindly
toward their mother. When she sees
me, she blinks once in the dimness
& heat. Blinks again when I don't
leave. The hay scratches a pink
pattern on my thighs.

[*in the woods*]

My brother tells me he almost stepped
on a fawn. She was sleeping across
his path & startled when he came
too close. I go looking for her
under every tree. Find prints
in the earth but not their maker.
Perhaps she has taken flight. Perhaps
the sky has swallowed her up.

[in the air]

My mother calls us all inside
before dark, the dusk rising,
coming up over the horse path.
It's spring. The lilac bush swallows
one side of the barn & the air
tastes thick with blossoms.
I count which of the robin's eggs
have hatched—which are still asleep.

I DREAM MY BROTHER TELLS ME HE WAS WRONG

& I don't know what to say even now that I'm awake & morning is coming through blinds like flood waters. It's raining on the East Coast today & I'm in a drought,

far from home or anything that tastes mountainous or ferned: that moss throating of greenery. When I was little my brother worked construction, came home

with sinewed muscles, stocky & sunburnt. I hung off his arm, made him carry me through the woods behind our house. A small explorer with bodyguard. This was before.

The after began with a thinning in our phone calls. After I ran into him on my way to our small town's first pride parade & there was a sound like breath holding

itself too long & it stayed in my chest long after. Now he builds homes for people with the same rolling hills, makes screened-in porches for family dinners in summer

& we haven't spoken in two years, find less & less in common even when I am home drinking beer at our parents' house under the maple trees. A souring branch leaning over the back porch. I know all the wingèd seeds are falling there today, helicopters dropping down into puddles, floating on the surface for a moment before they sink.

BEREAVEMENT RATES

There's a ghost in the corner of the room
& my cat can see it. He blinks twice
to say he's scared away
the stowaway mice. I blink once

to confirm. I've never lived in my own
house before. Moved from apartment
to apartment, state to state. Now I'm here
trying not to disrupt whatever is haunting
the air conditioner. I am my own type
of specter, bring along my baggage:
my grief cataloged & pressed into curtains.

I bought my first couch on Saturday.
Went to the store & picked it out—asked
about financing. I wanted to pretend
this was normal for me. That I've always been
able to point & have but the words tumbled
from me before I could stop them: *this is
my first couch / I've never bought a couch before.*
The woman working smiled & went on
processing my credit card as if I hadn't
admitted to something we both knew I had.

When I flew home for my sister's funeral I had to ask
for a bereavement rate from the airline. A discount
seat for grieving on a puddle-jumper plane.
There in the dark of five a.m. I felt the air shake
around me like rocks in a shoe. Heartbeat turbulence.
Can of Canada Dry Ginger Ale sweating itself
into my palm-grip. Who deserves
what they actually get? I'm afraid my house knows
I don't deserve anything I have.

If I die on this goddamned flight, how
will my family afford a second wake?

I am still making excuses to the house, to my cat
—tell them how hard I've saved. Explain
my history of terrible wanting & hand-me-downs,
the brown paper bags of government surplus
foodstuff. My own crooked teeth in the mirror.

I decide to hide the throw pillows in the closet.
I decide to tell my ghost the couch is secondhand.

I DON'T KNOW HOW TO TELL YOU THAT YOU DIDN'T PREPARE ME FOR THE REAL WORLD

once a man watched me from his truck

        I felt the translucent fish meat of me

the tenterhooked bones

        on ligaments

            under skin

the way the pavement undressed my kneecap

    a blood-red blossoming   I hate

how clumsy   my body is when it feels afraid

    how could I possibly fight   or flee

on these legs   these watered thighs

my trick knee

    is the only thing I inherited   from my father

this unruly joint   never staying

       where it should   saved him from the draft

                                          but only made me fall

it never stopped him from finding a war

                               I know what it means

to let go of

                 what holds you together

                                          & abandon balance

THE HEARTTHROBS OF MY GIRLHOOD

are playing serial killers now & if I'm being honest this is not a surprise. Everything I knew about desire was zipped into a being-looked-at-ness, the surveil of an undone dress or slipped shoulder bra strap. What I wouldn't have given to be appraised by boy eyes! How I cried & cried when a stranger on the internet said I was too fat/ugly to get raped. I watched Edward Cullen[1] sneak into Bella's house night after night to yearn for her unconscious body. Wished he would come into my bedroom, too. The imagined romance of blood lust following my dreams. I'd settle for anything, Troy Bolton[2] watching me sing the final number in the school musical. Waiting to catch me alone around a corner, to take me somewhere private. I was so ready at 15 or 16 to ruin my life for anyone looking in a rearview mirror or glancing over my shoulder while I wrote in my diary I wonder if anyone really sees me?[3]

---

[1] Robert Pattinson played Edward Cullen in the *Twilight* films. More recently, he played a predatory pastor and rapist in *The Devil All the Time*. Just like in *Twilight*, the age and power disparity between the two characters in *The Devil All the Time* is significant.

[2] Zac Efron played Troy Bolton in *High School Musical*. In 2019 he also played Ted Bundy in *Extremely Wicked, Shockingly Evil and Vile*. Chad Michael Murray also played Bundy in 2021 in *Ted Bundy: American Boogeyman*. I first saw Murray in *A Cinderella Story* in 2004 playing opposite Hilary Duff.

[3] Even now, when my husband watches me undress before bed, I have to remind myself to look back.

II.

How Do You Get It Back

EVERY TIME I HAVE A BIRTHDAY & SYLVIA PLATH DOESN'T

Too many women wear pale dresses & then die.
I cannot unmarry the two now: the thrill of femininity

on a delicate backhand, the starless & fatherless & the O
-mouthed slap of hurt. I wish the moon never changed

her face so people would stop talking shit about the ideal
of impermanence. Its corseted good looks.

There are so many poets I worry will die young. I worry
about dying of something pretty. I don't need anyone

eulogizing my under-ripe casket, my un-cobwebbed
body. [If you're not thinking of Snow White, you should.

How will you know you're girled. Do you remember
that Ophelia dies offstage. We only love her after picture.]

Let's look at this another way:

I watched a ghost show where the women who died
had costume changes written in. Wore flutter-sleeved

gowns to their own hanging. When the wind blows, maybe
it will still look like we are dancing. Why should the word

epitaph sound so alluring or soft when it is a stand-in
for all possibility. The infinite hush of past tense.

I'm looking for roundness again in all the wrong
places, the arc of a satisfied breath

but the moon is just a young slip of a girl tonight.
She writes poems, then eats them. Her autopsy finds

the remains. Thank god, we were able to save her.

TWO MONTHS AFTER MY SISTER'S FUNERAL, I WAKE

to ask my husband if he believes in ghosts.

He tells me: *not like that* or *no* or *I don't know.*

I can't remember what he tells me.

It's night & I have been dreaming

terrible things. Now I can't sleep at all.

At the funeral they told me *everything*

happens for a reason & *a better place now.*

I keep dreaming her here, at home.

Where else would she have gone?

I didn't know I'd lost god until he didn't

make me feel better. The hospital staff did

all they could, I guess. There were tubes

& I wasn't there. The church was full of tasteful

candles. Flowers. A wedding, but backwards.

We buried handshakes in our sleeves.

I was there for that part. I remember it

less than I should. Remember the cold cut lunch

afterwards perfectly. Dozens of pink meats

folded like napkins. The superfluous greenery

nobody eats. What did they do with the leftovers?

Maybe someone named Linda or Mary bagged it

up. Told a friend *well, waste not, want not.*

I want the morning to come but hear night sounds:

My husband falling asleep around my body.

The heater kicking on.

I dream her home again &

again she knows she's dead.

I WANT TO SAVE YOU FROM YOURSELF BUT INSTEAD I WRITE POEMS ABOUT AN ANIMAL SWALLOWING THE SUN WHOLE

Perhaps you know this one: there is a beast or lion-other
the sounds of it snake through the forest
outside my house. Sometimes it sounds like dogs
left hungry. The story diverges here: perhaps
the beast is good, animaled by reputation alone.
Perhaps it is the one leaving bones at your door.

I stay perfectly calm in a crisis. I can be still,
I can stop my heart beating on command.
This makes me harder to smell—the slowing
blood-pumped flesh of me.

Tell the story like this: once there was a broiling
summer & the beast had to hide in the shade
of a tree. The sun was too hot & the animal
was impatient for the cool of night. It unhinged
its jaw & breathed in until tongue hissed
against the sun rock, then swallowed it.
Gullet surprise & ripening. Fur bristle.
The night came on like a light & made my eyes adjust.
What is an ordinary amount of rage. How to ladle
yourself into smaller & smaller bowls.

I don't remember if I am the sun or the stomach
lining or the forest bearing a quiet witness.
Which is most to blame. No one knows
how to end a ballad so they return to the chorus.
There are new meanings every time you return to.

I heard an animal in the forest when I was little
& have not stopped listening for it since.
The trees tell me to tell it again.
& this time, pay attention: tell it right.
What color was the sun through the animal
hide. How do I get it back.

ON SEEING ONE BABY SHOE IN THE ALDI PARKING LOT

I buy a pumpkin for 99 cents a pound / count my change at the register like communion wafers / twice blessed / my husband sees twins everywhere / asks if their parents need both / we pack groceries into our car / gently / I say of course & don't believe myself / I don't go to church anymore / hang Saint Dymphna over my desk instead / the patron saint of the nervous / the lost & the losing / what if I take / the shoe from the parking lot / offer it to her image / token or barter / I know better / fall comes over the hills sweating & coppered / the trees cast in a creeping bronze / the shallow-belly breath of Oklahoma farmland / I leave / the pumpkin outside to swelter / Dymphna catches a beam / from our headlights / there & then gone

SUGARING SEASON

In March, the trees have bucket houses nailed
into them, like doorknobs for giants
—something fairy-worlded into my own.
I am five, or seven, or nine. I can't remember.
My sister says she remembers little
before seventeen. We are missing wire or string,
connective tissue for girls who grew up
in the woods. I can hear the trees dripping, sipping
delicately on air, making sweet. The snow,
still thick, forms a perfect buttonhole of earth
around each trunk. Bark peels where woodpeckers
have been knocking. My nose is cold
from trying to smell spring coming. Wind as hard
as an unripe olive presses against me.
The trees remember how old I was/am
—keep score of knobble-knee stride. I can't
wait to taste sap, bubbling in my mother's pot
spooned hot into my mouth. Mothwing light.
I remember this. I remember the swallow
and warm. My mother keeping our home
through winter.

IF I HAVE A DAUGHTER, I WILL CALL HER *SHIPWRECK*

to remind her that she is a remains.   Not the action

but the ghostyard   the coming upon after.

I need her to know that she did not cause   the trouble waiting

for her when she slides into my arms   out of my control.

My mother always reminds me to keep forgiving
                              everyone who has hurt me

even if they are hurting
                    me still. She was raised by a mother

always apologizing.
              We are a strand of pearls knotted by *it's okay,*

I don't mind. But that stops with mine: my daughter:
imagined. Peeling into the world like warped wood crying

into the arms of my body   of water. Insisting on
                        the brokenness around her.

If I have a daughter I will call her *Rabbit Hair*
                        or *Thistledown*, or *Flotsam*.

Whatever gets caught   in the teeth and curls in the throat.

She will be what refuses   to be swallowed.
                                                    The whole of my moon:

stubborn and shivering.   I have nothing to make her from
                                          but   conjure her

from whatever I can spare: some string, a thimble or anchor

the way my mother   says *wait*.

WHEN A STRANGER CALLS THINKING I'M HER SISTER

she leaves a message on my voicemail
saying our brother has died. It happened
last night. She'll call later with the details.

How to tell her I am the wrong
listener, the wrong grief? When I do,
I say I'm sorry she has my number

instead of her sister's, that their brother
has died after weeks in hospice. I mean:
I'm so sorry for this intrusion on your sorrow.

I am embarrassed by the intimacy of her
ear pressed to phone as she thanks me
for calling, her quick breath close to mine.

I am embarrassed by my own awkwardness,
say *god bless you* even though I don't know
what it means to be blessed after your brother

is dead. Somewhere in New York
there is a gathering of birch trees burnished
gold in an October sun. My siblings & I used

to play there. My brother would make
tall shadows along the grass like a giant
—something fleeting or frightening.

On the phone I tell this stranger
to *take care* as if we've known each other.
As if I could walk through my old backyard,

through the trees & knock on her back door.
Offer her a branch to hold onto, sunlight
still clinging to my outstretched hand.

UNSAYING GHOSTS

After my aunt dies I drive my mother home
from St. Louis to New York. Find Pennsylvania a never
-ending stretch of barely greened

trees & overpriced hotels. We stop
for continental breakfast, sunrise eggs
& burnt coffee. I can't remember now if

we share a bed, who puts down her credit
card first. I only remember our grief riding
shotgun. The way my mother told everyone

for weeks what a good driver I was, how
confident I seem in busy traffic. She doesn't
relay how the brake lights in the car ahead

of us fail & I nearly crash into a bumper on Ohio
highway. How my hands shake on the steering
wheel for hours after. It's too easy to think about

fragility: how the women in my family are prone
to osteoporosis: sharp tongue corrosion. Calcium
supplements for breakfast. The way a body

can start to eat herself after she's carried
too many people. In the car I let my mother

choose the music, her fingers perch on the dial

of the radio. She searches for a station
with a clear connection. No static, no ads.
Something to last the rest of the way home.

UNSAYING MY OWN HEART

A golden shovel for Anne Carson

Oh mirror, once I caught you
looking at me. Remember?
At the time, I wanted too
much from gazing. Too much
from unsaying my
own heart. Learned from mother
how to be a folded voice box. Said:
I am nothing. Star-eyed to
a fault. Did it hurt me
to be a flowered thing. Recently,
I feel brambled. Thorned. Why
do I have to hold
everything in my bones. Latch onto
the feminine art of all
or empty. I think that
may be what killed my mothers and
their mothers, forever. I—
still pulling thistle tongues—said
I will find out where
we've been hiding our throats. I can
see them, pink and glinting. I
won't stay put
now that I can imagine it:
sound floating on air like down.

SHELL WITH BOG & GHOST

Imagine you are a hermit crab, only you
have lost your shell-home & now use
anything small enough to steal away on foot.

Walnut or creamer-cup. Bottle cap or leaf.
As you sleep, the edges of your borrowed house
pinch your skin. You cannot return or rest or fold

your legs around yourself like a prayer.
This is how grief feels, you tell your remaining
sisters. There are parts you can't find

your way back to, everywhere there is a terrible
irritation: the sounds of another day burning
your theft hands, sand stuck between cartilage

joints. Your unborn daughter, only possible,
listens inside her own temporary shell
—curled in on herself, a seahorse buoyed

against coral. You know she hears you
burying a mother you might have been.
You've already ransacked another home.

SELF-PORTRAIT AS MY SISTER'S FRECKLE

I used to see myself as Girl: full time.
                   Persephone   pomegranate lips

& waist but I haven't looked   waif-like since I was 12.
      I remember
my blue dress over anxiously blooming   body.
                           The way our family friend

stopped me to tell me affectionately that I wasn't
                               a little girl anymore

& later I dreamed I was in love with him.
                           I didn't know what daddy

issues were then   just that I loved to be looked at
      like I was
             older than I really was   like
I still didn't pad my bras at home. This is

not what daddies are thinking but   my blue
                    dress didn't know any better.

I don't tell my husband all of this   I tell him enough
      for him to really know me. It has taken years to do this
           much: to tell instead of mime my needs behind glass:

sad smile puppet shadows along our bedroom wall. Years
of being looked at taught me this much—Ursula the Sea Witch
telling me the importance of *body language* in her cave while I
watched, sea-star eyed, mouth a round, red, never moving *Oh*.

*

It's my aunt's birthday, 2021. She would have been
68 today & I find a photo of her on Facebook from when
she was my age—maybe younger. I confess: I need us to look
alike because it's the only way I have to know her. My strange
ingestion of her: becoming by chew & swallow. Freckle & lash.
You know, she & my mother are like twins despite their age
difference. Same eyes, same hair pull & twist gestures.
My mother is kind & I am like her in many ways or most ways
but I am something else, too, & I want to know if this is where
my aunt & I overlap: this bite of mine, this quarrelsome tooth.

>   When I saw my aunt for the first time in over a decade
>   she called me "bunny" even though I was 23 & I felt
>   loved/was so desperate for her love & I didn't
>   know why.

I don't know who in my family is best at loving
—it's not me but I might be best at asking for it.
As a kid I was adored—loved smiling at grownups,

knew what approval tasted like. As an adult
I have to relearn my needs. My longing to
be loved or else.

I have been writing this personal thesis statement
for too long—bringing it to my husband between
my teeth & under our sheets.

There is a possibility I am waiting for him to grow
tired of me, of my need for touch & assurance.
I need so much & this is embarrassing. I am

an embarrassment of needs. Just look at me!
White-whaling my skin along our bed
in our small small apartment.

*

How embarrassing—! All my poems become love poems
to myself. I can't stop confessing me to me & isn't that
love? I read the Bible a lot when I was young & I never
felt how I was supposed to. Somehow transcendent? Now
I listen to pop music & I do—I hear Megan Thee Stallion
& Cardi B tell a lover to *park his big mac truck right in this little garage*
& I know what it is to feel connected to forces beyond
yourself—call it divine & I'd believe you. A sort of immaculate
conception, an accessible miracle. This hip-rolling chorus.

I hate being the sole witness to my own symptoms. Prefer
    corroboration
or else complete secrecy, like how I never tell anyone that I think
    I might
turn into oncoming traffic someday—even if I don't really want
    to.
When my body is sick it is always strange, unseamly, or meal-
    mouthed

disease. The rash under my breast in college. The stomach pain
    & vomiting
that followed me from Ohio to Oklahoma, vanished &
    resurfaced. As a child

I had warts on my feet, cauliflower-blossoms on one heel. They
    left & returned

& left again. Even to me it seemed like I might have invented it
all.
Become hysterical over a mosquito bite & embellished lesion &
mass. Mistaken
heartburn for ulcer. Diagnosed myself easy & mysterious. Once
when I was 11

I found a lump on my un-become chest & the doctor told my
mother it was
a breast bud. A marker I suppose, that I could burst at any
moment—crack

into a new body like a saint covers her modesty with overgrown
hair.

I wake & my body has aged again—my skin silvering into 30
(don't call me dramatic my therapist told me
it is okay to feel my feelings).

What if we make a baby & she comes out like me—already old?

      I thought the first time I had an ultrasound they would be
listening
for a heartbeat. My husband holding my hand, both of us
breathless
Is it a girl? What should we name her? Is everything alive? Instead I am

alone & they are looking for a pain source. The doctor thought
I was exaggerating phantom ulcer from pizza grease or fat
but the technician counts ten as she maps my stomach—
ten gallstones laying flat along my organ. *If you tell me you're in pain,
I'd believe you,* she says. I know now I'm not Hera, not fertile & full
of trembling life—I'm Zeus. Stone-full. Swallowing
whatever tries to escape me.

*

self-portrait as a wide-mouth pot   hot burner/red simmer

    as a sunburn across your shoulder/as my sister's freckle

as plant in the window that grows against the light

    —which is to say/as turning object   moved off course

self-portrait as   someone else's dream

    self-portrait as tentative thesis statement   stop

overheating   stop overeating   put down the fork

    throw the pot into the snow

>When I was little I always got sunburn
>—would forget sunscreen or shade
>& lap up fervor of pale blue New York
>sky with abandon. Remember my mistake
>too late when my skin sizzled. Heat
>radiating off my body & into the twin
>bed my sister & I shared. Fevered
>like the sun had licked my wounds
>too roughly. Like I had ignored

                                        some kind of warning.

I should probably be thinking of Icarus now, but I'm thinking of
    Persephone again.

        Soft flower child.

                Bride by accident.

This is the sort of story I love[d]—ones about girls
in love(?) a little more complicated than necessary.

I don't know why

        or I do & it is something unsettling about sacrifice.

What were all the reasons I wanted to be Meg, from Disney's
    Hercules?

        You're saying too much, Roseanna.

        Roseanna, you're peeling away

& the resulting scab is tender & hideous.

My body is nearly 30 & suddenly things are going awry
        I schedule an appointment to have a man
        peer down my throat   collect samples
        & come back up for air

                        This is routine
 but sounds like magic

        like a submarine
        voyage or Amelia Earhart's plane

 A surface shimmering on a wet horizon

*

> I've been losing time in the bath lately.
> It's a small tub & I sit in the center
> —pull my knees to myself & listen
> for waves caused by my own gravitational
> shifts, my soft shy limbs. Suddenly
> I am my own moon.
> The silence & I eclipse.

I used to be jealous
of women who waxed

& then waned bodies
shedding their fullness

I only grow rounder
—wide like an open lip

a smile coming up over
teeth like a tide

I am always eclipsing.

> Roseanna, you drift when
> you get anxious.

> You are a wanderer.

This is why you can't stop watching ghost shows.

Or this is why you sit at the kitchen table & scroll
your phone for nothing.

Or this is why the plants in your front window
are dying.

    It's ghost logic: everything absent is open for haunting.

*

Want to know a secret? I miss platonic touch to my core.

There is nothing that makes me heartsick like seeing girls together.

Do you know what I'm saying? We all live so far now.

My sister & I suddenly this year can tell each other the truth.

I call her at least once a week—or she calls me & I can't stop telling her everything I am thinking.

She is the beautiful one. I am the nice one.
We plan our breaks from these names & others.

My sister has freckles all year long. Like the sun can't stop kissing her. She tells me she like me better now
that I am meaner.
I tell her I am sorry I raised her
& then moved away.

I call her to make sure she is still there. That she hasn't swallowed
too much air,
too much light, in her apartment 7 or 8 states away.

She calls to say she is bored, alone, painting again. I keep her on the phone late.

V, you'll never believe this, I say

Yeah? she says

Tell me something new.

ACKNOWLEDGMENTS

Versions of these poems have appeared in the following journals:

"Giving or Gutting" in *The Missouri Review*

"I Don't Know How to Tell You That You Didn't Prepare Me for the Real World" in *Moon City Review*

"Queen Anne's Lace" in *Blueline*

Roseanna Alice Boswell is a queer poet and educator from Upstate New York. She earned her MFA in poetry from Bowling Green State University and is currently working toward her Ph.D. in English-Creative Writing at Oklahoma State University. Her debut poetry collection, *Hiding in a Thimble*, was released with Haverthorn Press in 2021, and she was the winner of *Iron Horse Literary Review's* 2021 Chapbook Competition for her manuscript *Imitating Light*. Roseanna's research interests include feminist theory, fat studies, and how these two fields speak to femininity and domesticity. She lives, writes, and teaches in Stillwater, OK, with her husband and their cats.

www.ingramcontent.com/pod-product-compliance
Lightning Source LLC
Chambersburg PA
CBHW060541080526
44586CB00012B/815